How Shall We Travel?

GO Green

Helen Lanz

W
FRANKLIN WATTS
LONDON • SYDNEY

First published in 2010 by
Franklin Watts
338 Euston Road
London NW1 3BH

Franklin Watts Australia
Level 17/207 Kent Street
Sydney NSW 2000

Series editor: Julia Bird
Design: D.R. ink
Artworks: Mike Phillips

A CIP catalogue record for this book is available
from the British Library.

ISBN 978 0 7496 9275 9

Dewey classification: 388

Picture credits: Age Fotostock/Superstock: 11c; Kelvin Aitken/Alamy: 11b;
Yusef Anil Akduygu/istockphoto: 11b; Richard Baker/Alamy:27br;
Ed Berien/Shutterstock: 11t; Bettmann/Corbis: 7r; Craft Vision/istockphoto: 7b;
Jens Fisbaek/istockphoto: front cover b; Lynn Graesing/istockphoto: 27bl;
Grafissimo/istockphoto: 21b; Denise Hager/Alamy: 26;
Gavin Hellier/Alamy: 19b; John Henshall/Alamy: 7br; www..iwalktoschool.org: 17t;
Jupiter Images/Thinkstock/Alamy: front cover t; Shane Kato/istockphoto: 15t;
Brian Keen/Alamy: 9t; Morgan Lane Photographers/Shutterstock: 6;
Frank Leung/istockphoto: 15b; René Lorenz/istockphoto: 9b;
EGD/Shutterstock: 10; Gary Martin/istockphoto: 21t;
Steven May/Alamy: 24; Ian Miles/Flashpoint/Alamy: 16;
James Morgan/Shutterstock: 8l; Dmitry Naumov/Shutterstock: 17b;
Lindsey Parnaby/epa/Corbis: 11c; Alex Segre/Alamy: 18b, 20;
Joe Sohm/Alamy: 18t; Ray Tang/Rex Features: 23b;
Peter Titmuss/Alamy: 19t, 22t; Terry Whittaker/Alamy: 25b.

Every attempt has been made to clear copyright.
Should there be any inadvertent omission,
please apply to the publisher for rectification.

Printed in China

Franklin Watts is a division of Hachette Children's Books,
an Hachette UK company.
www.hachette.co.uk

To Jez - maybe stick to walking from now on.

"*During 25 years of writing about the environment for the Guardian, I quickly realised that education was the first step to protecting the planet on which we all depend for survival. While the warning signs are everywhere that the Earth is heating up and the climate changing, many of us have been too preoccupied with living our lives to notice what is going on in our wider environment. It seems to me that it is children who need to know what is happening: they are often more observant of what is going on around them. We need to help them to grow up respecting and preserving the natural world on which their future depends. By teaching them about the importance of water, energy and other key areas of life, we can be sure they will soon be influencing their parents' lifestyles, too. This is a series of books every child should read.*"

Paul Brown
Former environment correspondent for the *Guardian*, environmental author and fellow of Wolfson College, Cambridge.

Contents

Getting around   6

The rise of the car   8

Travelling the world   10

Hotting up!   12

A necessary trip?   14

What about walking?   16

On your bike!   18

Go public!   20

Reduce car use   22

Planet-friendly travel   24

Going the distance   26

Glossary   28

Useful information   29

Index   30

Words in **bold** can be found in the glossary on page 28.

Getting around

How did you get to school today? Did you go on a bicycle? Maybe you walked? Many of your class will have travelled by car, some, perhaps, by school bus. It's unlikely that any of you went by plane!

Lots of children travel to school every day on a school bus.

Transport

As we move from place to place, within our village, town or city, or between countries, we use different forms of **transport** to get around. We can choose to walk, cycle or to go by car, bus, tram, boat, train or plane.

Early travel

Until the second half of the 20th century, people did not often travel far. Cars were too expensive for the average family, and air travel was not common. If people did go abroad, they usually went by ship.

After World War I (1914–1918), technology that had been developed for fighter planes was used to improve air travel. In June 1939 there was the first 'commercial' flight, for general air travel, from New York, in the USA, to Marseille in France.

Passengers on the first round-the-world flight, 30 June, 1947.

Eating food gives us the **energy** to move around.

Travel and energy

All travel uses energy. Travelling on foot and cycling use our body's energy. Our energy comes from the food we eat, so we need to make sure that we have a hearty breakfast before we set off! All other forms of transport use fuel, most often **petrol** or **diesel**, to make them go.

The rise of the car

Can you estimate how many cars there are where you live? Does every house have a car parked outside? And how many houses are there near you? Nowadays, most households, particularly those in **developed countries**, have one or more cars.

Developed vs developing

The top ten countries for car ownership are all developed countries. In the USA, over 140 million people – that's almost half of the total **population** – own a car. In the UK, there are around 31 million cars, and in New Zealand, nearly everyone old enough to drive owns a car! People in **developing countries** are less likely to own a car, as cars are expensive to buy and maintain. Car ownership in developing countries is growing fast, though.

There are over four times as many people in China as in the USA, but in China there are about nine million cars compared with over 140 million in the USA. ➡

TO THE MOON AND BACK

If all forms of passenger transport in the USA were lined up, bumper-to-bumper, they would reach from the Earth to the moon and back. The fuel needed to run all these vehicles for one year would fill a swimming pool the size of a football field and 64 km deep!

THE GREAT BRITISH CAR PARK

It is estimated that by 2031, there will be 33.5 million cars on the roads in the UK. If all these cars were parked at the same time, they would fill a 52-lane motorway from London to Edinburgh. That's about 650 km!

Many people choose to drive to out-of-town shopping centres rather than visit shops in their local area.

Car lifestyles

Nowadays, people in developed countries don't often think about how much they rely on their cars to get around. Even how we arrange our towns and cities shows how much we depend on cars. For example, it is now common to have out-of-town shopping centres that you need a car to reach. In some countries, such as Australia and New Zealand, the distances between places are very great. Having a car makes it a lot easier for people to get around.

The longest highway in the world runs almost all the way around Australia and is over 20,000 km long.

Travelling the world

We don't just move about within our countries. Have you heard the expression that the world is now a 'global village'? This means that because of modern transport, it's now so much easier and faster to travel around the world that it feels as though we live in a small village.

With modern transport, travelling to far-off countries is much easier than it used to be.

Flying high

The fastest way to travel long distances is by plane. Planes can fly through the skies at over 900 kilometres per hour! There are around 200,000 flights around the world every day. That's over 8,330 flights every hour, 138 flights every minute, or over two flights a second. It can be exhausting just thinking about it!

Train travel

To travel shorter distances, many people choose to travel by train. For example, about 4.8 million people a day travel on underground trains, using 26 lines from 468 stations, in New York alone. Trains can also travel longer distances, though at a much slower rate than by plane. You can travel under the sea on a train from the UK to France through the Channel Tunnel, or from one sea to another, from the Indian Ocean to the Pacific, across Australia.

It's over 4,300 km from Perth to Sydney by train across Australia's Nullarbor Desert. It takes around three days.

Ship ahoy!

And it's not just people who move about. Nowadays, goods (the things we buy) are often made in one country and sold in another, so we move goods from one country to another all the time. Things can be moved by ship, or flown by air. Most goods tend to go by ship because this is cheaper. In fact, there are about 50,000 cargo ships from over 150 countries used to transport goods of all kinds all around the world.

About 90% of the world's goods are transported by ship.

Hotting up!

All of this travel takes a big toll on our **environment**. The explosion in car and plane journeys in particular has been linked with both **global warming** and **climate change**.

Fossil fuels

In order to work, cars, most lorries, trains and planes need petrol, diesel and oil. These are known as **fossil fuels**. Fossil fuels are formed under the ground over millions of years.

When fossil fuels are burned, they release energy and this makes cars and other vehicles move. However, when the fuels are burned, they also release a gas called **carbon dioxide** (CO_2).

Global warming

2. CO_2 is a greenhouse gas, one of the gases in the Earth's **atmosphere** that trap the Sun's heat. As more fuel is used, more greenhouse gases are added to the atmosphere. This means that more heat is kept in, warming the Earth up.

3. Rising temperatures have started to change the weather patterns around the world. This is called climate change.

1. Coal, oil and gas develop underground over millions of years. When they are burned, they create energy. Burning these fuels gives off carbon dioxide **emissions**.

Global warming

Earth's climate varies naturally, but evidence shows that people have made it change more quickly by burning more and more fossil fuels. One effect of this is a gradual increase in Earth's temperature. Out of the five warmest years on record, four have occurred in the last ten years.

Extreme weather

We can already see the effects of climate change, with extreme weather patterns forming all around the world. **Heat waves** and **droughts** are becoming more common in some areas, while rainfall can be very heavy in others, causing flooding. Extreme weather events, such as hurricanes, are also increasing around the world.

Cracked earth in the USA and flooding in the UK show the effects of climate change around the world.

Did you know?

Driving a car for 5,000 km or flying between London and Moscow four times creates one tonne of CO_2 – the same weight as a fully-grown, female walrus.

13

A necessary trip?

Luckily, there is a lot we can all do to help reduce how our journeys affect the environment. Firstly, we can all try to cut down on the number of journeys we make by car.

An elephant a year

Everyday journeys by car contribute 13% of all CO_2 emissions in the UK. On average, each UK car gives out 2.4 tonnes of CO_2 into the air each year. In the USA, the average car releases about 4.6 tonnes into the air each year. That's nearly an elephant's-worth of CO_2 for every car every year! So people who have cars cannot just blame air **pollution** and global warming on other people – they all play a part.

Use it less!

We need to start thinking about whether we need to use our cars as much as we do. Here are some simple things to think about each time you and your parents or carers are about to get in the car:

Can you
- save up chores and do them all together to reduce the number of journeys?
- share a car journey with a friend or neighbour?
- choose not to go in the car? Is the errand close enough to travel on foot, by bike or on **public transport**?

 Taking the bus to school is better for the environment than going by car, but walking is even better!

Lighten the load

Travelling 24 km less each week in our cars would reduce our carbon emissions by 408 kg a year. That's saving the same weight in CO_2 per person as the weight of two American black bears. Remember, in the UK, there are over 31 million cars, so that would save over 62 million bear's-worth of CO_2 from going into the air each year.

 Imagine if we all saved a couple of bear's-worth of CO_2 each year – that adds up to a big saving.

15

What about walking?

One way we can cut down on our car journeys is by walking more. Did you know that nearly a quarter of trips we make by car are less than 3 km in distance? That's less than a half-an-hour walk.

The Walking Bus

Would it be possible to walk to school from where you live? Many schools around the world have a 'Walking Bus'. This is where authorised adults stop at agreed 'bus stops' on a well-used route to school, to 'pick up' children to walk them to school in a group. Walking is good for you and, as the only fuel you use is your own energy, it's good for the environment too!

In a walking bus like this one, there is always an adult 'driver' and some other adult 'conductors' to make sure the children are safe.

Walk around the world

There are international schemes such as WOW – walk to school once a week – that aim to get children walking to school. In October, there is an international walk to school programme where children from all around the world join together in that week to walk to their school. In 2007, a record 42 countries took part to make it a more 'walkable world'.

Make sure you have permission from your parent or carer before you go out for a walk.

CASE STUDY

THE WONDERS OF WALKING

Walking regularly is a great way to keep your body fit and it is one of the safest forms of exercise. It helps to keep your heart, lungs and muscles in good condition, it strengthens your bones and it also helps to control your weight. What's not to like?

On your bike!

Did you know that for the **natural resources** and energy it takes to make one car, you could make about 100 bicycles! Once it has been made, it is your energy that makes a bicycle work, not the Earth's.

⬆ A bicycle is 30 times less expensive to buy and keep going than a car.

Journeys of less than 8 km, and those in built-up areas, are often quicker on a bike than in a car.

Fit and planet friendly

Travelling by bike is a great way to keep fit. It doesn't put strain on your body, but it gives your heart and muscles a good work-out. If you are travelling in a town, it can often be quicker to travel by bike than to go by car because many roads have lanes that only buses and bicycles can use. And as the only energy you burn when cycling is your body's, the only CO_2 emissions from cycling is the air we breathe out!

Did you know?

You can travel up to four times faster on a bicycle than you can by walking, using the same amount of energy.

Cycle safely

It is very important that you only cycle with your parents or carers. Be sure to wear a well-fitted cycle helmet and ride on a bike that is roadworthy. If you are cycling on or near roads, you should wear the correct reflective clothing so that cars and other vehicles can see you clearly.

Regular cycling is a great way to stay active and fit, but make sure you have the right equipment before you set off.

CASE STUDY

A CYCLING NATION

The Netherlands sets a good example of how to encourage more people to cycle. It has spent millions of pounds on developing good cycle paths, with separate traffic signals for bikes. Often, the bike has right of way over other transport on the road. The Netherlands has a population of 15 million people, and 12 million bikes!

This bike park is by the main train station in Amsterdam, the Netherlands.

Go public!

Sometimes, it's just not possible to walk or go by bike because we need to travel too far. But don't jump in the car just yet! Have you ever thought about going by public transport?

Bus, train or tram

Some of us have got so used to relying on our cars that it wouldn't cross our minds to catch a bus or train to go somewhere. Did you know that in the UK, 89% of people (that's most people) live less than a six-minute walk away from a bus stop. So what's stopping us from getting on the bus?

Can you drop me at the bus stop?

Bad name

Unfortunately, public transport can sometimes have a bad name as trains or buses often run late, or are too crowded at peak travel times. However, many people think that if more of us use public transport, and demand that it is run better, it will have to improve.

 In the USA, families living near public transport links drive, on average, 7,080 km less per year.

Here are some things we can all do to help improve how we use our local public transport services:

- get up-to-date timetables for your area; look out for special deals, and try to book in advance for a cheaper price
- ask your parent or carer if you can use public transport instead of the car for a few regular journeys. Plan them very carefully. Try and make these regular changes to your week's travel
- when public transport is poor, write to your local MP.

Buy train tickets in advance to save money on your fare.

CASE STUDY

GET ON BOARD!

By train, plane or car? Or coach? Of all these ways to travel, the coach is the most environmentally-friendly way to go. This is mainly because coaches transport a lot of people in one go. Research shows that coaches release just 0.03 kg of CO_2 per passenger-kilometre. This is half what trains give out, and much smaller than the amount given out by cars (0.11 kg) and planes (0.18 kg). So get on board!

One full coach in the USA can take 55 cars off the road.

Reduce car use

Sometimes, travelling by car is simply the most convenient and efficient way to get from A to B. But there are ways of making travelling by car more environmentally friendly.

Car sharing

If your journey to school is too far to walk or cycle, perhaps you could talk to your parents or carers about sharing the car journey. Do you live near a classmate? Perhaps you could take it in turns to make the journey by car? But remember – your safety comes first. Car sharing should be a proper arrangement made by your parent or carer.

Did you know?

A standard car will produce its own weight in CO_2 once it has travelled about 9,600 km. That's usually within a year.

No son, car share means we share journeys, not that you can 'share' my car whenever you like!

SHARE THE STRAIN!

People working for the same company or in the same town or city can join a car pool, where they share their journey details and then team up with someone who lives near them to share lifts. One car-pooling scheme in the city of Leeds in the UK estimates that it saves over 4,800,000 km of car travel a year. That's over 120 times around the circumference of the Earth. Now that must have saved both fuel and CO_2 emissions!

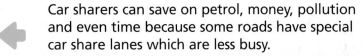

Car sharers can save on petrol, money, pollution and even time because some roads have special car share lanes which are less busy.

Go eco or electric

If your family needs a new car, why not choose an eco car or an electric one? Eco cars produce far fewer CO_2 emissions than traditional cars and there are now many models available. Alternatively, you could buy an electric car, such as the popular G-Wiz. Electric cars run on electricity rather than petrol, and are powered by a rechargeable battery. Electric cars still produce CO_2 however, as fossil fuels are burned to produce the electricity that powers the cars.

Did you know?

Nearly one third of all car mileage in the UK is clocked up by people travelling to and from work.

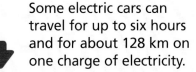

Some electric cars can travel for up to six hours and for about 128 km on one charge of electricity.

Planet-friendly travel

Air travel is one of the biggest causes of air pollution and makes a big contribution to global warming. With over 200,000 flights a day worldwide and an average plane using 4 litres of fuel per second, it's not hard to see why. So it's important to think about different ways of travelling long distances when possible.

Flying facts

Each day, there are about 1.8 million passengers in the sky over the USA on one of the 24,600 flights that travel over America.

All models of the Boeing 747 plane have travelled about 50 billion miles; that's the same as flying to the moon and back 75,000 times.

Greener holidays

In the UK, people take over 40 million holidays abroad each year. It is important that all of us, wherever we live, think carefully about how we can reduce our impact on the environment when we go on holiday. There are things that we can all do:

- take holidays within our own country to avoid flying or travelling far
- look into all the ways to travel, by train, boat or bus to see which is best
- support travel companies which are eco-friendly.

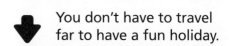
You don't have to travel far to have a fun holiday.

Carbon off-setting

We all have a carbon footprint. A carbon footprint trail is an imaginary trail that we leave when we use electricity, oil and gas in our homes, schools and workplaces, and petrol in our vehicles. Every time we use a 'carbon' energy (coal, oil or gas), it gives off CO_2. Organisations that have a large carbon footprint, such as big companies, can 'off set' this carbon by helping to look after the environment. They can do this by donating money or 'carbon credits' to organisations that carry out projects all over the world to reduce the amount of CO_2 that goes into the air.

We each have a carbon footprint. It is measured in tonnes of CO_2 released into the air.

Carbon credits can be put towards funding environmental projects such as wind farms, a source of 'clean', **renewable** energy.

Going the distance

To change how we travel, we must first change our habits. We can start simply, by changing just one journey we make each week. If we keep it simple, we are more likely to make the change last.

Walk into the record books

Many of us can walk to school. Find out when the international walk to school month is, and help take it into the record books by joining the millions of people who are already taking part. Who knows? Walking to school may become another good habit! And it will keep you fit as well as being good for the environment.

 Small things can add up to make big ones. If we all make one journey less by car a week and walk or cycle instead, that adds up to a lot less CO_2 going into the air.

FUTURE FUELS

We are never going to stop travelling completely, so scientists are developing new types of fuel.

Green electricity, sourced through renewable energies such as wind, solar and tidal power, will provide more of our electricity in the future. This will make the electric car a much greener type of transport.

Biofuels are an alternative fuel to petrol. They are made from plants that are burned to produce energy. They cancel out the CO_2 they make when they are burned by using up CO_2 as they grow. However, some people think that biofuels use up land that should be used to grow food, and that they create different types of pollution.

Another form of energy is hydrogen fuel cells. This is where the chemicals hydrogen and oxygen are combined in the fuel cell into water, producing electricity. This electricity can be used as power, instead of petrol, for example.

Plug in to recharge and then off you go!

This plant makes biofuel from grain.

Glossary

Atmosphere The layer of gases that surround the Earth.

Biofuels Fuels made from plant matter.

Car pool An arrangement when people who work together or live nearby share their cars to get around.

Carbon dioxide A gas in the air.

Climate change Long term changes to the world's weather patterns.

Developed countries Countries with well-developed economies, where most of the population work in factories and businesses.

Developing countries Countries with less-developed economies, where most of the population work in farming.

Diesel A fuel made from oil that is used to power cars and other vehicles.

Drought A shortage of rain over a long period of time.

Emissions Substances, such as the gas carbon dioxide, that escape into the air.

Energy The power to make or do something.

Environment Surroundings.

Fossil fuels Fuels such as coal, oil or gas, which have developed under the ground from rotting animal and plant life over millions of years.

Global warming The gradual heating up of the Earth's atmosphere.

Heat wave Unusually hot weather in an area over a long period of time.

Natural resources Materials, such as water and wood, that are found in nature.

Petrol A fuel made from oil.

Pollution Making something, such as the air or water, dirty.

Population The number of people living in a place.

Public transport Vehicles, such as trains and buses, that follow set routes at set times for people to use to get from one place to another.

Renewable Something that is in constant supply and will not run out, such as the wind.

Tidal power A type of energy produced by harnessing the power of the tides of the sea.

Transport Different types of vehicles, such as cars, buses, aeroplanes and so on, used for carrying people or goods from one place to another.

Useful information

Throughout this book, 'real life measurements' are used for reference. These measurements are not exact, but give a sense of just how much an amount is, or what it looks like.

Walrus = 1 TONNE

Asian elephant = 5 TONNES

American black bear = 200 KG

Earth's cirumference at Equator = 40,000 KM

Average distance from Earth to the moon = 384,500 KM

Further reading

Earthwise: Getting Around by Jim Pipe (Franklin Watts, 2008)

Action for the Environment: Transport Solutions by A. Gilpin (Franklin Watts, 2006)

Websites

www.ctc.org.uk
The website for the International Walk to School organisation.

www.celebratingcycling.org
All about cycling.

www.care2.com/channels/ecoinfo/transportation and

www.roadsafetyweek.org/educators/web-centre/in-the-classroom/websites-for-primary-school-children
Lists websites with information about transport and the environment.

Dates to remember

Earth Hour – 28 March

Earth Day – 22 April

World Environment Day – 5 June

Clean Air Day – June

Walk to School Campaign – May and October

World Food Day – 16 October

Buy Nothing Day – 28 November

Index

air travel 7, 10, 11, 24

Australia 9, 11

bicycles 6, 15, 18-19, 20

biofuels 27, 28

boat 6, 24

bus 6, 15, 18, 20, 24, 28

car 6, 7, 8-9, 12, 13, 14, 15, 16, 18, 20, 21, 22-23, 26, 28

car pools 22, 23, 28

carbon dioxide 12, 13, 14, 15, 18, 21, 22, 23, 25, 26, 27, 28

carbon emissions 14, 15, 18, 23

carbon footprint 25

carbon off-set 25

China 8

climate change 12, 13, 28

coach 21

cycling 6, 7, 18-19, 22, 26

developed countries 8, 9, 28

developing countries 8, 28

diesel 7, 12, 28

electric cars 23, 27

electricity 23, 25, 27

energy 7, 12, 16, 18, 25, 27, 28

fossil fuels 12, 13, 23, 28

fuel 7, 8, 12, 16, 23, 24, 27, 28

gas 12, 25, 28

global warming 12, 13, 14, 24, 28

greenhouse gas 12

holidays 24

Netherlands 19

New Zealand 8, 9

oil 12, 25, 28

petrol 7, 12, 23, 25, 27, 28

planes 6, 10, 11, 12, 21, 24, 28

pollution 14, 23, 24, 27, 28

public transport 15, 20-21, 28

ship 7, 11

trains 6, 11, 12, 20, 21, 24

tram 6, 20

UK 8, 9, 11, 13, 14, 15, 20, 23, 24

underground trains 11

USA 7, 8, 11, 13, 14, 15, 20, 21, 24

walking 6, 7, 15, 16-17, 18, 20, 22, 26

walking bus 16

World War I 7